from:

Believe in Yourself

Written and compiled by Beth Mende Conny
Illustrated by Donna Ingemanson

PETER PAUPER PRESS, INC.
WHITE PLAINS, NEW YORK

Illustrations copyright © 2001
Donna Ingemanson

Designed by Heather Zschock

Text copyright © 2001
Peter Pauper Press, Inc.
202 Mamaroneck Avenue
White Plains, NY 10601

ISBN 978-0-88088-558-4
Printed in China
35   34   33   32   31

Visit us at www.peterpauper.com

In matters of love, family, friendship, and work, this collection of thoughts encourages you to take control of your life and ideas, to turn life's stumbling blocks into stepping stones.

As you turn these pages, take the words of advice to heart and mind. Let them serve as loving, accepting, tell-it-to-you-straight kinds of friends. Seek their counsel and their wisdom. Most of all, let them serve as your mirror, reflecting the special person you are and will always be.

B. M. C.

Let's dare to be
ourselves,
for we do that
better than
anyone else can.

SHIRLEY BRIGGS

There is only one real sin
and that is to persuade
oneself that the second
best is anything but
second best.

DORIS LESSING

When your mind is
full of indecision,
try thinking with
your heart.

The greatest revenge is to accomplish what others say you cannot do.

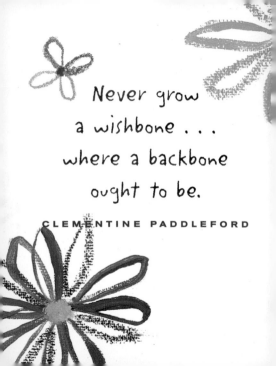

Never grow
a wishbone . . .
where a backbone
ought to be.

CLEMENTINE PADDLEFORD

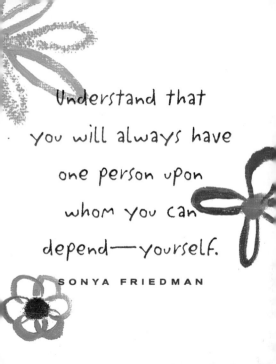

Understand that
you will always have
one person upon
whom you can
depend—yourself.

SONYA FRIEDMAN

And the day came
when the risk to
remain tight in a bud
was more painful than
the risk it took
to blossom.

ANAÏS NIN

Take your life in
your own hands,
and what happens?
A terrible thing:
no one to blame.

ERICA JONG

Remember: you are
the only person who
thinks in your mind!
You are the power
and authority
in your world.

LOUISE HAY

The past was.

Tomorrow may be.

Only today is.

faith is the

cornerstone on

which all great

lives are built.

One of my rules is:
Never try to
do anything.
Just do it.

ANI DIFRANCO

Don't be frustrated by
your inexperience—
all green things
inevitably grow.

Sound the note
that calls your
soul to you.

SANAYA ROMAN

The answers will come if you're there to greet them.

Be courageous.
It's one of the
only places left
uncrowded.

ANITA RODDICK

If the future seems overwhelming, remember that it comes one moment at a time.

Self-acceptance gives
you the much-needed
energy and freedom
to grow.

If you don't know
the answer, perhaps
you should rephrase
the question.

Be like the
birds—
sing after
every storm.

Let your dreams

be your

North Star.

Should you meet
resistance, take
comfort—it's a great
way to build muscle.

If you don't take control of your life, don't complain when others do.

Expect trouble as an inevitable part of life and when it comes, hold your head high, look it squarely in the eye and say, "I will be bigger than you. You cannot defeat me."

ANN LANDERS

Don't regret what
might have been.
Accept what is and
rejoice in what is
yet to be.

Let old dreams
fade into the night,
so new ones can rise
with the dawn.

Maybe we will turn
from the horoscope page
to the Congressional Quarterly,
and understand at last that
our salvation lies not in
our stars, but in ourselves.

NAOMI WOLF

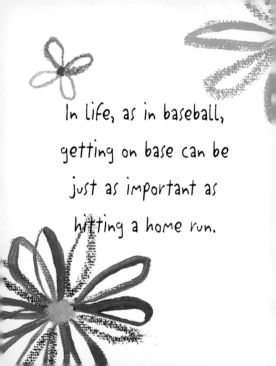

In life, as in baseball,
getting on base can be
just as important as
hitting a home run.

Remember, if you
don't want to
be with yourself,
why should
anyone else?

SONYA FRIEDMAN

Don't forget

the three R's:

rest, replenishment,

and reflection.

What ultimately holds true is that the better a woman's self-esteem, the more likely she is to find a satisfying relationship—and the more she likes her looks, no matter how close or far they are from the beauty ideal, the better her self-esteem is likely to be.

CAROLYN HILLMAN

Don't wait
for the world
to change.
Change it
yourself.

follow your heart
the way sailors
follow the stars.

Knowledge is a
salve that soothes
many a fear.

If at first you
don't succeed—
try setting more
realistic goals.

Do great things in your life, but do small things as well.

Live today fully and you create a lifetime of meaningful memories.

Don't strive to be
better than others,
strive to be
your best self.

Being busy doesn't

necessarily mean you

are being productive.

Being alone is scary,
but not as scary
as feeling alone in
a relationship.

Some of us have great runways already built for us. If you have one, take off! But if you don't have one, realize it is your responsibility to grab a shovel! Build one for yourself, and for all those who will follow you.

AMELIA EARHART

Never give up,
for that is just the
place and time that
the tide will turn.

HARRIET BEECHER STOWE

When old habits
are hard to
break, try
bending them.

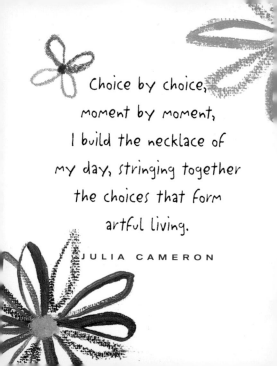

Choice by choice,
moment by moment,
I build the necklace of
my day, stringing together
the choices that form
artful living.

JULIA CAMERON

There are no impossible dreams, just our limited perception of what is possible.

Listening requires
the use of our
hearts as well
as our ears.

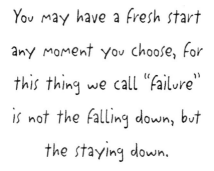

You may have a fresh start
any moment you choose, for
this thing we call "failure"
is not the falling down, but
the staying down.

MARY PICKFORD

Patience is a skill,

perseverance an art.

[Y]ou have to pay close attention to what you love, and never listen to anyone who tells you to be practical too early in the game.

BARBARA SHER

A sense of humor,
like a true friend,
sees you through
bad times.

The richness of human
experience would lose
something of rewarding
joy if there were no
limitations to overcome.

HELEN KELLER

Sometimes the most
forceful statement
you can make is
to remain silent.

Don't avoid a good argument, just a bad one.

If you can't change

your fate, change

your attitude.

AMY TAN

To make up for
lost time,
commit to living
in the present.

You don't need
a loud voice to be
heard. All you
need is something
worthwhile
to say.

Apologize,

don't agonize.

Nothing in life is so
hard that you can't
make it easier by the
way you take it.

ELLEN GLASGOW

It is in the company
of a good friend
that the heart
finds a home.

There are no mistakes,
no coincidences. All
events are blessings given
to us to learn from.

ELISABETH KÜBLER-ROSS

Sometimes the hardest thing to do is to do nothing at all.

falling's part of the game. It's like my dad always says: "No matter how good you are, the ice is still slippery."

MICHELLE KWAN

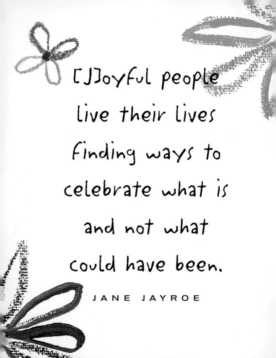

[J]oyful people
live their lives
finding ways to
celebrate what is
and not what
could have been.

JANE JAYROE

If you want
Lady Luck in
your life, open a
door for her to
enter.

Know your limits,
not so that you can
honor them, but
so that you can
smash them to pieces
and reach for
magnificence.

CHÉRIE CARTER-SCOTT

You can't
change that
which you
can't accept.